THE COST OF IGNORANCE

Also by Robert Phelan

Broke:
The Broken Contractor's Insurance System
and How to Fix It

Secrets of Peak Performers
(with Dan Kennedy, Bill Glazer,
& Lee Milteer)

THE COST OF IGNORANCE

What You Don't Know
About Performance-Based Insurance™
Can Save Your Company Millions

ROBERT PHELAN

Voxie
MEDIA

The Cost of Ignorance
What You Don't Know About Performance-Based Insurance™
Can Save Your Company Millions

Copyright © Robert Phelan 2013. All rights reserved.

Published by Voxie Media
Big Ideas. Short Books.™
voxiemedia.com

CATALOGING-IN-PUBLICATION DATA IN PROGRESS

ISBN 978-0-9886203-0-8

Printed and bound in the United States.
First printed January 2013

The paper used in this book meets the minimum requirements of the American
National Standard for Information Services—Permanence of Paper for Printed
Library Materials, ANSI Z39.48-1992

Book design by Alex Miles Younger / alexmilesyounger.com

To my father, who introduced me to the insurance business and taught me to be dedicated to my client's success.

CONTENTS

ACKNOWLEDGMENTS

First, I want to thank my clients, past and present. Without the challenges they put in front of me, I never would have mastered the esoteric concepts presented in this book.

I'd also like to thank Doran Lamond, one of my senior associates at Litchfield Insurance Group. Working closely with such a talented insurance professional has helped me tremendously in refining the concepts of Performance-Based Insurance™ or PBI™. Her dedication to our clients and her eagerness to learn PBI in all its forms has helped them greatly.

Thanks to Rich Ducci and all his associates at Ducci Electrical Contractors. As our longest tenured PBI client, we have worked with them to examine every form of PBI invented. They have challenged us and stretched our capabilities. It is clients like this to whom we owe our deepest gratitude.

Our biggest leap into the more challenging concepts of PBI began when we met the group captive experts at Captive Resources (CRI) in 1995. Founder George Rusu and his team literally created this concept and have introduced it to thousands of middle market businesses across the U.S. Group captives have saved their participants hundreds of millions of dollars over the last quarter century. Thank you, George, for encouraging our participation in the distribution of CRI's group captive products.

Most recently, we expanded our PBI portfolio to include the Series LLC captive concept. Thanks to Doug Deitch and Cindy Burks from Keystone Risk Partners for their patience and the considerable time they spent in educating us and our clients on the benefits of the captive structure.

PBI concepts are not confined to the world of captives. Even though that is the focus of this book, our traditional insurance carriers offer a wide array of PBI alternatives. The Travelers, The Hartford and AIG have all provided PBI products and services to a wide range of our clients over the years. Without their partnership many of our clients would not have benefited from PBI. Thanks to these carriers for their commitment to PBI and the millions of dollars they have saved our clients.

For the last fifteen years, my mentor and coach has been Roger Sitkins, founder of Sitkins International. His influence on me and my company has greatly influenced our success. We would never be where we are today without his wisdom and encouragement. Thank you, Roger.

This project began innocently enough with an online course whose goal was to write an eBook for Kindle. That course was taught by Debbie Weil, founder and CEO of Voxie Media. She took my rough manuscript and turned it into the book you hold in your hands (or on your e-reader). She went from online instructor to become my editor and publisher. It is due to her endless encouragement and belief in this project that I was able to complete it. Thanks so much, Debbie, for your tireless dedication to me and to my book.

If you've opened this book, I'm sure it is partly due to the provocative cover. Thank you, Alex Miles Younger, for lending your great talent to this project. Without a doubt, this is the best cover ever designed for a book about insurance.

PREFACE

The story you're about to read has a bracing narrative and is full of drama. But it's really about middle market businesses and how they buy insurance. Now, don't be disappointed.

The insurance industry is not the enemy some believe it to be. Having been in the insurance business my whole career, I find it fascinating. My love for this industry and all it is capable of motivated me to write this book. The book is also driven by my belief that we practitioners need to do a much better job communicating how insurance works—and how it can work better for everyone.

Our industry uses confusing, jargon-filled language to describe "Alternative Risk Transfer" or ART. What does that mean? Essentially, it means you are buying an insurance policy that is variable in cost depending on the individual claim performance of the insured entity—your company. I have created a new name for ART in all its forms. That name is Performance-Based Insurance™ or PBI™. Hence the subtitle of the book: if you perform well, you pay less and can save millions.

As you go about your day, it's likely you don't think about the role of insurance in our culture. But life as we know it would come to a standstill without insurance. No money would be lent, no construction projects started, no workers employed, no homes and factories built or purchased, nor boats or cars. No development of new life-saving drugs. Nothing.

It's because the risks of ownership and of liability are too great for any of us to operate without insurance. Even if we thought we could handle the financial risks ourselves, the government, the financial institutions, and other third parties demand that any potential claim payments are guaranteed by a third party with very deep pockets. Simply put, having insurance is essential to running our global economy.

Worker safety and wellness lie at the heart of what my company, Litchfield Insurance Group, does. Too often, I have seen lives and families ruined by death and disability caused in the workplace. Safety can no longer be viewed as a "nice to have" extra, provided only if it's convenient. Rather, promoting safety—and its cousin, wellness—needs to be a core strategic initiative for middle market companies that aim to thrive well into the 21st century.

Although the safety and wellness concepts presented in this book apply universally, some of the other concepts aren't necessarily right for every company. For many reasons, conventional insurance may always be a company's best option.

In addition, the concepts introduced here as alternatives to conventional insurance only apply to certain types of coverage. They happen to be the ones in which large premiums are spent, like workers' compensation and health insurance. However, with hundreds of coverages and policies on the market today, the majority are purchased for a fixed, guaranteed cost—and most likely always will be.

Although the philosophy I espouse is a valid one, you'll see that I generalize about several insurance industry practices. Please take some of the narrator's commentary with a grain of salt. When characterized in the extreme, some of the industry's nonsensical behaviors make for better reading. Feel free to laugh with me. At the same time, listen closely to the underlying message.

I'm not asking you to love the insurance industry as I do. If I did, you'd probably close this book right now. But you might grow to like the PBI concept presented in this story, especially if you can actually own a piece of your own insurance company.

Love insurance or continue to hate it, that's your choice. But I guarantee that your view of insurance will never be the same after you read this book.

Robert Phelan, ARM
CEO, Litchfield Insurance Group
Torrington, CT
www.litchfieldins.com

PROLOGUE

Tim and Julie were having another one of their Sunday evening fights about money. Always Sunday because that's when Julie paid the bills.

Tonight was particularly painful because the subject was the final college tuition payment for their son, Tony. He was in his last semester, and they had only half the funds they needed.

It was early fall and Tony was due to graduate in December. Tim had promised Julie he would be able to deposit more money after his company's re-financing was complete.

Unfortunately, with the depressed economy and tight credit, Tim's credit line had actually been reduced rather than expanded. He knew he should have told Julie, but he'd been hoping the company would land a new client that would generate a substantial amount of cash.

Julie was beside herself. "How did you let this happen!?" she demanded. "Every time I asked you about it, you said we'd be okay. What on earth are we going to do? Tell Tony that after four years of hard work he can't graduate?"

"Of course not," Tim replied indignantly. "I've always been there for you and Tony, and that's not going to stop now."

"Oh, you mean like you were there for us when we had to skip our family vacation for the last two years in a row?" Julie responded, raising her voice. "Or when you took $200,000 out of our retirement plan to buy new trucks?

JULIE WAS BESIDE HERSELF. "HOW DID YOU LET THIS HAPPEN?" SHE DEMANDED.

"And what about your employees and their families who've depended on you? How many have lost their dreams because of your layoffs?"

"Okay, okay!" Tim threw his hands up with resignation.

"Look—it's been a tough couple of years. Who could've predicted that the economy would stay in the tank for so long? My company's not the only business in tough shape."

But Julie would have none of this argument. She'd heard it all before and was tired of the excuses.

"Maybe it's time to start working smarter," she shot back. "And I'm not so sure your yearly escape to that San Francisco conference fits into the *smarter* category. Why don't you give it up this year—stick around and buckle down instead of going off to drink with your buddies?"

"But, Julie," Tim replied in his defense, "the conference is full of smart people with good ideas. Maybe I didn't take it as seriously as I should have in the past. This year I will. I'll come back with a winning idea that'll make things better around here. I promise."

Julie was adamant. "I'll give you a week, Tim. One week. That money better be in the bank by next Sunday, or you and I are going to have a big problem."

Tim nodded with determination, but a knot was forming in his stomach. Leaving the table, he escaped the tension-filled atmosphere and walked out the sliding glass doors onto the deck and into the brisk autumn night. The fresh air was a relief, but it couldn't suppress the question in his mind: Had he just made a final mistake in Julie's eyes, betting everything on the conference?

AND WHAT ABOUT YOUR EMPLOYEES AND THEIR FAMILIES WHO'VE DEPENDED ON YOU? HOW MANY HAVE LOST THEIR DREAMS BECAUSE OF YOUR LAYOFFS?

CHAPTER 1

At 30,000 feet, Timothy Franculli settled in to the drone of the plane, gazed out the tiny window, and reflected on the past year—one he hoped never to repeat. He'd owned his wholesale food company for 25 years, most of them good ones. But the last year had brought the perfect storm of bad news.

It all started in January with an increase in employee health insurance rates of 15 percent, or $180,000. Then, in April, he lost his biggest customer and 25 percent of his revenue to a national competitor due to lower prices. This led to layoffs and a renegotiation of his line of credit.

Company morale had never been lower.

Then came more bad news. A series of employee injuries the year before caused his workers' compensation premiums to skyrocket 40 percent in June. That meant an extra $200,000 the company didn't have. Fortunately, his long-term banker provided cash. That cushioned what could have been a financial disaster. But if his plan to acquire new customers through a private label division didn't work . . . well, he didn't even want to think about that.

The private label division was a make-it-or-break-it bet for his company. He couldn't really afford it, but his customers were demanding the new service. Even if it were successful, he would need more cash to ramp up. If only he could find a way to reduce those monthly insurance payments. . . .

Tim broke his reverie and turned away from the window. He leaned back in his seat (coach, not business, unfortunately) and closed his eyes, trying to block out the negative narrative. After all, he was headed to San Francisco and his favorite annual gathering—with high hopes for discovering a solution there.

Five years ago, he'd joined a group of about 100 owners of medium-sized businesses from around the U.S. They had been meeting once a year in San Francisco to discuss innovative ideas, industry trends, and other subjects that could help grow their companies. Main-stage events were followed by breakout sessions on a variety of topics. Each year's conference had a theme, and this year's would be financial strategies for growing companies—hardly surprising.

HE NEEDED A MIRACLE—OR AT LEAST AN INNOVATIVE IDEA TO HELP HIM REDUCE INSURANCE COSTS.

In truth, despite a lingering sense of guilt over Sunday night's conversation with Julie, Tim was happy to be getting away. Last year had been such a grind. At least temporarily, he could put the day-to-day details of his business behind him and focus on the big picture.

Consultants always said owners should be working "on" the business, not "in" it. But putting out fires had been his life for the last year. Thoughts and plans for the future had all been postponed. He hoped that over the next few days his peers would provide ideas to reinvigorate him. He needed a miracle—or at least an innovative idea to help him reduce insurance costs.

The World Series was fast approaching, and for a moment Tim thought about baseball, his passion since he was a boy. He felt like a pitcher standing on the mound late in the 7th inning. The problem he faced? His best pitch wasn't working, and the bases were loaded. His team was two runs behind and the count was against him. He needed to dig deep and find a winning focus.

* * *

The San Francisco baggage claim area was crowded with rumpled-looking passengers. As he was jostling for position near the belt, he looked around and saw a familiar face.

"Bill? Bill Sullivan? Hey! I haven't seen you in forever."

"Timothy Franculli! I'll be damned. It's been ages—since the LaRosa Foods dealer meeting in the early '90s, right? Wow, it's great to see you! How've you been?"

"Oh, pretty good . . . but there's always room for improvement," Tim replied, smiling at his friend. Miraculously, his bag appeared on the belt directly in front of him. He snatched it up. Then he quickly moved to the other side of the belt to shake hands with Bill, a tall, impeccably dressed man in his late 40s.

"So what brings you here from Florida?" Tim asked.

"I'm speaking at a conference for middle-market companies over at the St. Regis," Bill replied.

"Not the Centennial Group by any chance?" Tim queried.

"Yeah—that's the one. How'd you guess?" Bill sounded incredulous.

"I've been a member of Centennial for five years now. That's where *I'm* headed. Same meeting. So you're speaking to our group?"

"Yes, I'm one of the main speakers. And I just joined, too. My sponsor heard my story and thought I had something interesting to share with the membership, so he asked me to give a talk. I thought, 'why not?' Frankly, I'm not sure how new my information will be for your group. You're a smart bunch."

WE BUY INSURANCE THE OLD-FASHIONED WAY. TO BE HONEST, IT'S KILLING US RIGHT NOW.

"So what are you speaking about?"

"It's a unique type of insurance program my broker introduced me to 20 years ago. My company has never been the same since. No way we'd be where we are today without PBI—that's Performance-Based Insurance. Saved us more money than I ever could've imagined. Changed our culture, too. I'm always surprised that more businesses haven't heard of it. You have PBI, right?"

"Um, no," Tim admitted. "I'm not familiar with PBI. We buy insurance the old-fashioned way. To be honest, it's killing us right now."

"Hey, there's my bag," interrupted Bill as he reached down to grab his suitcase. "Want to share a cab? I can tell you more about PBI on the way to the hotel."

"Sure." Tim scanned the terminal and pointed to the right. "There's the taxi stand right over there."

As they walked to the cab, Tim thought about how lucky he was. The conference hadn't even started yet and here he'd met a friend—one of the conference headliners, no less—who seemed to have a cost-cutting idea related to insurance, his biggest problem.

But even though Bill was an old friend, Tim still had his doubts. He wanted to believe Bill had a magic solution, but he'd fallen for similar ideas before. Insurance is a mysterious business. PBI. Why hadn't his broker told him about this new kind of insurance?

Tim glanced at Bill, a guy who sure looked prosperous. Fancy leather bags. Probably flew first class. Tim felt a little embarrassed about his old nicked-up American Tourister. But he was excited. Really excited. Maybe Bill was about to share an idea that would save his company. His intuition had told him to go anyway—and, boy, was he glad he listened to it.

Bill and Tim jumped in the cab, and it immediately roared off toward the City by the Bay.

PBI. WHY HADN'T HIS BROKER TOLD HIM ABOUT THIS NEW KIND OF INSURANCE?

CHAPTER 2

As he and Bill settled into the back seat after their long flights from the East Coast, Tim was eager to learn more.

"So tell me about this PBI . . ."

"Hold on, old friend," said Bill. "Let's catch up a little before we talk business. Tell me about what's happened in your life? I think we started the same year as management trainees for Rondo back in '82, then we both went off on our own in '87, I believe. You to Charleston and me to Miami."

"Good memory," replied Tim. "I bootstrapped myself with all my savings in '87 and carried just one line at first—LaRosa. For a while, I added another couple of lines and another couple of trucks nearly every year. Then I added produce and got into organics a few years back. Now we're developing a private-label line of products. I have 100 employees, a 100,000-square-foot warehouse, 30 trucks, and a lot of headaches."

They both laughed.

Tim added, "And last year was the worst year in our company's history. Other than losing our largest customer, our biggest financial problems are related to insurance.

"So tell me what you've done with your company, Bill."

"Just like you, we started with next to nothing in '87. That's when we hired good salespeople and the company took off. After five years, I had 75 employees and we'd just built our first warehouse. We're still headquartered in Miami, but now I have 600 employees and five warehouses throughout Florida.

"Business has been off a little with the economy, but life is good overall. I've got a great management team, and I'm starting to cut back my hours. I'm not ready to retire, but I *could*. In reality, I could retire tomorrow."

Wow, Tim thought. I guessed right. Bill's doing extremely well. How could we have started in identical circumstances—yet Bill is succeeding and I'm so buried in problems? Well, good for him. Now maybe I can learn new tricks before it's too late.

LAST YEAR WAS THE WORST YEAR IN OUR COMPANY'S HISTORY. OTHER THAN LOSING OUR LARGEST CUSTOMER, OUR BIGGEST FINANCIAL PROBLEMS ARE RELATED TO INSURANCE.

"That's fantastic, Bill," Tim said with sincerity. "It sure sounds like you could teach me a few things. Can we start with PBI? Insurance is such an issue for me. I'm eager to hear how you've solved it."

"Performance-Based Insurance. Where do I begin? But first tell me a little about your existing insurance program. How much do you spend? What's your experience been like?"

Tim sighed. "We used to spend about 400,000 dollars a year, but last year it went up to 600,000 dollars. My broker told me it's because my loss ratio was 80 percent and my experience mod rose to 1.45. Half the time, frankly, I don't even understand what he's talking about. It comes across as all 'smoke and mirrors' and I end up paying more money."

"Ouch!" Bill exclaimed. "I haven't had a one-year increase like that since before switching to PBI. That must have hurt."

"Hurt? It completely blindsided me," Tim blurted out in frustration. "That's one of the things I hate about insurance. You can't budget for it. The companies always have *some* reason it goes up. It just seems to bite you in the ass when you least expect it."

Bill empathized. "I can remember when that happened to me," he said. "It was my fourth year in business. That's when I was plowing all my profits back into the growth of the company. My agent came in with a 100,000-dollar premium increase completely out of the blue. I got stuck paying it that time, but I vowed it would never happen again. I began to research alternatives and that's when I found PBI. I bet that over the last 20 years, PBI has saved me 3 to 4 *million* dollars."

"Holy shit!" shouted Tim. "You must have really beaten up your agent and the underwriters to save that kind of money."

"You sound like someone who goes out to bid on your insurance every year," Bill responded.

"Of course I do. How else do you keep these guys honest?" Tim showed his disgust. "I keep trying to figure out this insurance game." He then affirmed that he'd pinballed from carrier to carrier yearly, always in search of that ever elusive cheaper premium.

Bill was quiet. Then he turned to his friend and asked, "Would you believe me if I told you I haven't gone out to bid in 20 years, and that going out to bid could be what's *causing* your premiums to rise so high?"

Tim looked perplexed. "How could that be?" What Bill had just said contradicted everything Tim had ever believed about business insurance.

Just as Bill started to answer, the cab pulled up in front of the hotel.

"Well, I guess you'll have to wait until my presentation in the morning. I'm on at 10 o'clock."

With that, Bill jumped out of the cab, grabbed his bags, and yelled, "See you for cocktails."

Tim still felt astonished. "Yeah. Sure. See you later," he muttered. All he could think was, *How does a guy save 3 to 4 million dollars on insurance and never go out to bid?* He decided to search for this PBI thing online when he got to his room. There *had* to be a catch. No way he could've missed something *this* big.

HOW DOES A GUY SAVE 3 TO 4 MILLION DOLLARS ON INSURANCE AND NEVER GO OUT TO BID?

CHAPTER 3

By the time Tim got to his room, he realized that the opening reception would begin in 30 minutes. He quickly googled PBI and saw no hits listed. Just what he figured. Probably a quirky gimmick that wasn't even legal. He didn't think Bill would break the law, but he didn't know him *that* well—and it had been 20 years. However, the search diminished his enthusiasm and deflated his mood. Oh well. Two days to go. He was sure he'd still get plenty of new ideas for reviving his company at this conference.

About halfway through the reception, he saw Bill standing by himself. Tim figured it was hard for any new guy to break into this close circle of friends. After all, some of them had been in Centennial since it started 30 years ago. So he walked over to see if he could introduce Bill to someone. He was still intrigued by the PBI concept, but he didn't want to bring up business if Bill wanted to relax and enjoy himself.

Bill saw him coming and met him halfway. "Hey, Tim. I didn't mean to run away from you before, but I was late for a conference call. It was our weekly safety meeting and attendance is absolutely mandatory, even for me. I'd say the safety of our workers is our most important cultural value. It started when we first introduced PBI and has gotten stronger ever since. No one on our leadership team misses the weekly safety meeting unless they're on vacation."

"Wait a minute" replied Tim. "You said that PBI stood for Performance-Based Insurance. What's safety got to do with insurance? At my place, safety means keeping OSHA off our back."

"I don't mean to sound critical, but that's where a lot of business owners have it all wrong. Didn't you tell me earlier that your workers' comp had gone up because you had a number of expensive claims? Without a strong cultural emphasis on safety, how is that going to change? When people get hurt and the insurance company spends money, guess what. You pay more. It's that simple. Not only that, but an unsafe workplace leads to morale problems, lost productivity, rehiring and retraining costs, and a host of other things we call the 'indirect costs' of employee injuries.

WHEN PEOPLE GET HURT AND THE INSURANCE COMPANY SPENDS MONEY, GUESS WHAT. YOU PAY MORE. IT'S THAT SIMPLE.

"In addition," Bill cautioned, "when you change carriers or brokers every year to find the cheapest insurance, you're unwittingly increasing the long-term cost of accidents and injuries, and you're potentially exposing yourself to an uncovered claim. That could be crippling.

"Three reasons are at play here. First, the discontinuity from changing carriers could leave you with serious coverage gaps. If you're only focused on price, you're missing coverage. Second, every carrier has different capabilities on claims. A claim worth 10,000 dollars with a strong carrier could spiral out of control and end up costing 100,000 dollars with a weak carrier. And third, you're likely not investing in safety, which is the only long-term way to lower your insurance costs."

Bill continued. "Tim, can you tell me how many lost-time injuries you average annually?"

Tim felt embarrassed. Obviously, Bill thought he should have this answer in his back pocket. So he looked down and mumbled, "I'm not sure. I'd have to call HR."

Bill responded, "Don't you discuss those figures at your safety meetings?"

Now Tim wished he could run and hide, but he gave an honest answer. "Truthfully, Bill, I've never been to one of our safety meetings."

It didn't appear Bill meant to put him on the spot because he looked uncomfortable, too. The he quickly let his colleague off the hook. "Tim, I didn't mean to embarrass you. I know companies who haven't been introduced to PBI aren't likely to focus strongly enough on safety. Hell, that's the way *I* was before the concept was introduced to me.

"In the old days, I concluded that employee injuries were a cost of doing business. I'm lucky I had a great insurance broker who introduced me to PBI early in my career. He's the one who got me to understand the importance of safety.

"Now, why don't we put this whole thing aside for tonight? When you hear my presentation tomorrow, you'll have a much better idea how PBI works. Then before we head home, I'll meet with you one on one and answer any questions you might have. Deal?"

"Sounds great, Bill. I look forward to it. Enjoy the rest of your evening."

Tim drifted into the crowd and ended up on the terrace as the sun was setting over the bay. Certainly a beautiful evening, but this PBI thing nagged at him. His insurance broker came from a big regional firm with an excellent reputation. Had these agents been taking advantage of him all these years? Everyone in town says they're the "go-to" guys for business insurance. Yet here Bill's talking about safety and this mysterious concept of PBI that no insurance guy had ever discussed with him.

As he thought about his company's P&L, the issue began to eat away at him. Bill is saving *millions* while my budget for insurance just keeps growing and growing. Why am I the one standing in the dark? Have I been getting bad advice—*so* bad, it could cost me my company?

Not surprisingly, he tossed and turned a lot that night. He had visions of Bill spending his days relaxing with his family while he toiled away trying to save his company, hoping he could retire while he was still young enough to enjoy it. That 10 a.m. presentation couldn't come soon enough.

HAVE I BEEN GETTING BAD ADVICE—SO BAD, IT COULD COST ME MY COMPANY?

CHAPTER 4

Tim was one of the first in line for registration the next morning. Although his concerns and questions had kept him from sleeping well, he was excited about the day ahead. In particular, he couldn't wait to hear Bill speak.

He grabbed food at the breakfast buffet and found a table with fellow members he knew. After quick hellos, the conversation returned to the owners of two manufacturing companies who were comparing their incredible successes. Tim became sullen and quiet, recognizing he had no "braggables" of his own. In fact, he felt like an outright failure. Distracted by thoughts of what awaited him back home, he excused himself to claim a seat for the first main-stage presentation.

He found a place in the second row and began perusing the program for the next two days. He noted that Bill's presentation on PBI was scheduled for the main stage, not a small breakout room. Tim had been skeptical when Bill told him he'd be a main speaker, especially when a search for PBI turned up nothing on the internet. But here it was—main stage! Now his interest was highly piqued.

The day began with an outstanding presentation by one of Centennial's most successful members, a software entrepreneur who had just attained "Inc. 500" status for the fifth year in a row. His current ranking: #31. His topic: "Maintaining Cash While Funding High Growth." The speaker told a great story and Tim picked up a few ideas to share with his CFO, but because his company hadn't enjoyed high growth for a long time, he had to admit, most of the concepts didn't apply.

After a short break, people returned to their seats to get ready for Bill's talk titled "Performance-Based Insurance: An uncommon and simple strategy to pay less than you ever dreamed for business insurance."

Bill's sponsor introduced him as a new member with an exciting idea. Tim knew that insurance was a big-budget item for many of the members; thus, this wasn't the first time an insurance idea had been presented. Still, he looked around and saw lots of anticipation on the faces of his colleagues.

MODERN INSURANCE BEGAN IN LONDON IN 1688 AT EDWARD LLOYD'S COFFEE HOUSE.

Bill provided his own brief introduction, saying, "Just like you, I own a medium-sized company. I happen to be in the wholesale distribution business, and my company has five warehouses and 600 employees. We're based in Miami and all our business is in Florida. In the early stages of our rapid growth, we developed insurance problems. My presentation this morning is about the technique I used to solve these problems, save my company, and free up a lot of capital for growth.

"I don't know any of you or what your businesses look like, so I'd like to start with a few questions. With a show of hands, who spends more than 150,000 dollars a year for property and casualty insurance?" With about 90 people in the room, probably 50 to 60 hands went up. "Keep your hands up," Bill instructed. "How many of you think you have an outstanding safety record or a good loss experience?" About half the hands went down. "For those whose hands are still up, how many of you get money back at the end of the year if you have low claim levels?" All the hands went down. "Wow," said Bill. "I thought *some* of you may have heard of my topic today, but I guess not.

"Well, let's get started. For any of you spending more than 150,000 dollars a year, this idea could work for you immediately. And even those who don't yet spend that much, I know you're successful entrepreneurs running growing companies. Someday soon you may be eligible, and you won't want to miss what I'm about to describe."

People began taking out notepads and pens. Tim already had his ready.

Bill continued, "A little history lesson to give my story perspective. Modern insurance began in London in 1688 at Edward Lloyd's coffee house. Of course, it's now known as Lloyd's of London. Ship owners would meet at Lloyd's and discuss their voyages. They realized the value of their cargo was great enough that it would be catastrophic to lose a ship at sea. Someone came up with the idea for the ship owners to share the risk. That way, they would subsidize each others' losses. A ship owner would write his ship's name and voyage and cargo on a slip of paper and post it in the coffee house. Other ship owners willing to share the risk would write *their* names under the ship's name. That's where the term *underwriting* came from. So from those modest beginnings, we now have a global insurance industry in which risk is shared among all the participants.

"Risk sharing is one of the key points in PBI," Bill went on. "Without it, insurance doesn't exist. And even more important for you, if your insurance premium doesn't transfer all or part of the risk to a third party, the IRS says you can't deduct for it. That means you can't pay money to yourself, put it in a different pocket, and call it insurance. Trouble is, once you pay it to an insurance company, a lot of your money gets used to pay other people's losses and not your own. Now, hold on to that thought; we'll get back to it.

"Before being introduced to Performance-Based Insurance, I was clueless about the insurance mechanism," he admitted. "Insurance was a black box where I deposited money, most of which I never saw again." Tim heard chuckles and saw heads nodding around the room. Bill had hit a sympathetic chord.

"What I'd like you to do now is think about Lloyd's of London in those early days. Essentially, a mini-insurance company was formed for every voyage. Ship owners sat over coffee and decided how they would share risk. Imagine if a ship owner or its captain were of questionable character. His peers would take very little risk to cover that owner's ships. If his reputation was solid, however, everyone would jump on board to share the risk. Of course, in those days, everyone in the coffee house knew the owner, the captain, and the risk they were taking. This is extremely different from the anonymity of buying insurance today."

Tim reflected on what Bill had said. Sure, at some level, he'd always known he was sharing risk with all the other companies that bought the insurance he did. But beyond that, the insurance world still seemed mysterious to him. He wanted more details about PBI.

TROUBLE IS, A LOT OF YOUR MONEY GETS USED TO PAY OTHER PEOPLE'S LOSSES.

CHAPTER 5

Bill still kept the audience's rapt attention. "The people who taught me about PBI separated the world of business insurance into two categories: those who bought PBI and those who bought Subsidy-Based Insurance or SBI," he said. "By your own admission with your show of hands earlier, all of you are buying SBI. Once again, SBI means Subsidy-Based Insurance."

People were taking notes but also looking at Bill quizzically. He'd just told them they were buying something none of them had ever heard of, namely Subsidy-Based Insurance. Murmurs ran through the crowd as the conferees looked skeptically at each other. All of a sudden, Bill was being seen as the "crazy new guy" instead of the insurance expert.

But Bill didn't appear rattled in the least. "Think about your workers' compensation for a moment," he continued. "With a show of hands, who knows the names of all the other companies with whom they share workers' compensation risks—similar to the ship owners in Lloyd's coffee house? Who knows the names of the other companies?"

No hands went up. Bill let everyone off the hook by saying, "Of course you don't. You pay your money to Travelers or The Hartford or CNA, and *they* figure out the companies you'll share with. Your money is safe and secure with them. You pay a reasonable premium, and they protect you when the unpredictable happens. Some years the claims hit you and some years, the claims hit the other guys. Over time, it all evens out."

Bill let that sink in for a minute and then asked, "But is that what you *really* want?" He let that question hang in the air and walked over to a whiteboard.

MURMURS RAN THROUGH THE CROWD AS THE CONFEREES LOOKED SKEPTICALLY AT EACH OTHER.

"Here's where the story gets more interesting. Let's compare these two forms of insurance—PBI and SBI." Bill then put the two headers on the board and drew a line down the middle.

Under SBI, he wrote:
Premium determined by market rates and others' experience

Under PBI, he wrote:
Premium determined by your own experience

"All of you who've been running companies for a while know that B2B insurance goes through market cycles. When the market cycle is soft, insurance is cheap; when it's hard, it's expensive. Sometimes really expensive. You can't control the cycle; the cycle controls you. Sometimes you're hit hard when you can least afford it." More grumblings from the audience. "What if I told you about a way to jump off that merry-go-round of up-and-down rates? Would you rather control your insurance destiny or have it controlled by outside forces?"

Next, Bill wrote in the SBI column: **Subsidize or be subsidized**

And in the PBI column he added: **Pay by performance**

"I'm not going to embarrass anyone by asking, but I know that statistically speaking, some of you are subsidizing and some of you are being subsidized."

WHAT IF I TOLD YOU ABOUT A WAY TO JUMP OFF THAT MERRY-GO-ROUND OF UP-AND-DOWN RATES?

Bill explained, "It costs roughly 35 cents of every premium dollar to run an insurance company. That's overhead. It pays for underwriters, actuaries, lawyers, claims personnel, marketing staff, and so on. That leaves 65 cents to pay the claims for the insurance company that breaks even. From the time the company collects your premium until all the claims are paid, it invests your money. In most years, the company is happy to break even on the insurance and make its money on investments. Not as much now with interest rates being so low, but over the long haul, that's been the formula.

"The problem with SBI is that claim payments aren't distributed equally to the policyholders. Yet within a fairly narrow band, they all pay the same premiums.

"How is that fair?" Bill asked rhetorically. "Shouldn't 'the good' be rewarded and 'the bad' penalized?

"Well, here's the way it works: *the good companies subsidize the bad.* Your insurance company takes the extra money you've paid that hasn't been spent and, because your losses are low, uses it to pay the claims of your competitors down the road—those who didn't pay enough to cover their own losses for the year. It's kind of like a Robin Hood 'steal from the rich to give to the poor' analogy.

"Let's use an easy example," said Bill. "Two construction companies each pay 200,000 dollars to Travelers. One has 50,000 dollars in losses and the other has 300,000 dollars in losses. Instead of returning the unused portion of the premium to the contractor with 50,000 dollars in losses, that premium is used to subsidize the contractor who was 100,000 dollars light. Multiply that example by thousands of companies in each insurance company's portfolio, and you get the picture.

"So how does the SBI model differ from the PBI model? Simple. The PBI model involves little or no subsidy. The insurance industry uses all kinds of jargon to describe the many different forms of PBI, but they all work the same way. You pay a fixed premium that goes to run the insurance company—whether it's Travelers, a mini-insurance company you form for yourself, or a small insurance company you form with fellow business owners, just like the Lloyd's example. Then you pay your own losses up to a point that works for you financially. You transfer the riskier and more expensive losses to the insurance company."

Subsidizing your competitors? Forming your own insurance company? Controlling your insurance destiny? All these concepts were foreign to Tim—and he still had no idea if they could save him money. All this insurance talk was wearing him down. If he could just get one solid, actionable, money-saving idea—and get it *soon* . . .

The clock was running, and he was running scared.

CHAPTER 6

Tim's head kept spinning with his problems. He had a huge line item called Insurance on his P&L every year, and *he wasn't sure what he was paying for*. Unfortunately, he didn't have to be an insurance genius to figure out his was one of the companies being subsidized. His agent had just explained to him that his premium didn't cover his losses and that's why his rates were going up. Now he'd probably learn he couldn't get PBI because his losses were too high.

"I'm sure you have a number of different questions at this point," said Bill, "and it will help everyone to hear the answers. I know you won't be a shy group. So ask away."

Hands shot up all over the room.

"Red shirt. Third row." Bill pointed to a participant.

"I spend about a million each year on insurance, and my agent has spoken to me over the years about captive insurance companies. Is that what you mean by PBI?"

"That's one form of PBI, and numerous other variations of captive exist, too," confirmed Bill.

"When he told me they're all based offshore in the islands, it sounded too much like a Bernie Madoff scam to me. Plus, my agent warned me it was quite risky," said the red-shirted participant.

Bill smiled. "I reacted the exact same way when I first heard the description of PBI. Fortunately, I had a broker who understood the concept inside and out, and he convinced me it was the *least* risky way to buy insurance.

"Here's why." Bill went back to the whiteboard. Under PBI, he wrote:

> **Little or no subsidy to others**
> **Control your insurance destiny**
> **Eliminate unpredictable premium swings**
> **You earn the financial rewards**
> **Eliminate the hassle of going out to bid**
> **Tax-deferred underwriting income**
> **Your experience determines your cost**

Under the SBI column, he wrote the opposite:

> **Subsidize your unsafe competitors**
> **No control of your insurance destiny**
> **Subject to unpredictable market swings**
> **Insurance company earns the financial rewards**
> **Constantly out to bid to keep system honest**
> **No underwriting income**
> **Everyone else's experience—even your competitors'—**
> **determines your cost**

Bill scanned audience members as they digested what he had just written. Then he asked, "Show of hands again. Who thinks PBI is riskier than SBI?"

Tim looked around and saw very few hands raised. The show of hands indicated about 80 percent thought PBI was *less* risky than SBI. Bill had made a good case.

HE DIDN'T HAVE TO BE AN INSURANCE GENIUS TO FIGURE OUT HIS WAS ONE OF THE COMPANIES BEING SUBSIDIZED.

"More questions?" inquired Bill. "You in the back row," Bill said, pointing to a young man who had stood up.

"On your whiteboard illustration you said to eliminate unpredictable premium swings. I've had really unpredictable swings as my Experience Mod has changed. How does that work with PBI?"

"Wonderful question," replied Bill.

"PBI gets you off the EMR (Experience Mod Rate) merry-go-round. This is particularly important right now because the EMR formula has just changed and if your experience is poor, the factor is going to be even more punitive. As most of you know, when you have a bad year, as every company does, your EMR will penalize you for the next three years.

Once that bad year is in the calculation, future EMRs are set in stone until that bad year falls off. Consequently, you have lost complete control of your workers' comp spend for three years. In the conventional guaranteed cost rating system there is absolutely nothing you can do to fix the problem other than control your claims so you come out in decent shape when the bad year falls off. We call this *The EMR Tunnel of No Return*.

"Contrast this with how premium is developed in a PBI. First of all, there is no EMR. Second, your premium is based on five years of loss data instead of three years so one bad year has only a 20 percent impact instead of a 33 percent impact. But those are the least important advantages. The most important is that PBI premiums have two components: the fixed costs to run the mini insurance company and the estimated cost of claims for the next twelve months. These factors are 40 and 60 percent of premium respectively.

"If you have a bad year, the 40 percent fixed cost piece doesn't change at all in the following year. The 60 percent piece for claims is adjusted upward to account for the one bad year out of five. But here's the good news and the big advantage for you. You're putting the 60 percent on deposit in your own account to pay for your claims. You have to put a little more in but it's *your money*. If you follow your bad year with a good year, all the unused money in your claim account is returned to you by dividend including any extra you put in because of the bad year.

"So instead of entering *The EMR Tunnel of No Return*, you have the ability to immediately recover. No three-year surcharge. No losing control of your premium cost. You're in total control of your insurance destiny and not subject to the arcane EMR formula that kills you for three years.

"Knowing how this works, if you qualify for participation in a PBI program, why would you ever stay in the conventional market and never have control of the one insurance cost that you *can* control?"

"In the guaranteed cost market, even though there is no EMR, insurance carriers penalize you in Auto and GL in the same way. And PBI works for you in those lines as well. So if you had the opportunity to control the three largest components of your insurance spend, why wouldn't you? I think it's a no-brainer."

A voice from the back of the room boomed, "If this is such a great idea, how come we've never heard of it before?"

It seemed as if everyone in the room was nodding. Intellectually, they understood the case Bill had made, but emotionally they still felt a lot of skepticism. Yes, why *hadn't* they heard of it before?

Bill smiled easily. "I always get that question early in the Q and A," he replied.

"I don't want to make this uncomfortable for anyone, but I have to be honest. Some of you are probably good friends with your insurance agent, yet these agents are a big part of the problem. As I've talked to many other PBI buyers over the years, I've basically concluded that your agent doesn't *want* you to know about or have PBI. Why? Because agents and brokers typically make less money on PBI products.

"Now, there are exceptions to every rule," Bill continued, "but most insurance agents do very little for their money. After the initial sale, their jobs involve processing the renewal once a year. And the service they provide during that year consists of reacting to your problems, not offering proactive assistance to help you avoid problems in the first place. Sure, they work to convince you they go to several markets and beat up the underwriters to save you money. But if that were true, they'd be out of business.

"You know why? Their whole business model depends on maintaining continuity of premiums to their insurance carriers. If they flipped around insurance accounts like pancakes every year, their insurance carriers would shut them down. So they go through the annual 'pretend bidding dance' to keep the incumbent carrier honest. It takes them very little time and effort. They should be *partnering* with the carrier to get you the most value, but many agents view carriers as adversaries and just beat them up at renewal time.

I DON'T WANT TO MAKE THIS UNCOMFORTABLE, BUT YOUR AGENT DOESN'T WANT ANYONE TO KNOW ABOUT PBI.

"On average, your agent gets 10 percent of the premium. If you pay 400,000 dollars a year, that's 40 grand in that agent's pocket. It's equivalent to the pay of a full-time employee in some markets and certainly that of a 50 percent employee in most. Tell me, do you think performing 'bid' work once a year is worth *that* much money? I don't think so.

"So what does this have to do with why you haven't heard of PBI?" asked Bill rhetorically. "Simple. Most PBI programs are based on a fee instead of a commission. Agents don't want to fully disclose their compensation, mostly because they know they don't earn it. It would be difficult to justify a fee at the same level as their commission. And why would they suggest an arrangement in which they're going to lose money?

"Another important reason you won't hear about PBI from your agent," he continued, "is that agencies receive something called contingency compensation from the insurance companies they represent. Each carrier has a different formula, but it's based on a combination of retention of business, new business, and profitability of business. Any account in a PBI program isn't included in this formula, even if the premium remains with the same carrier. Transferring large accounts to PBI could cost an agency hundreds of thousands of dollars a year.

"In addition, most traditional SBI insurance salespeople lose money on PBI and may even lose complete control of your account and all their commission. Some larger brokers move the PBI to a centralized unit where it's handled by specialists. Why? Because the administration of PBI involves a level of complexity that the staff of an average agency wouldn't understand. I've simplified the concept here because, at its core, it *is* simple."

The picture was becoming clearer for Tim. At least this might explain why his agent hadn't told him about PBI. However, it still wasn't clear whether he could take advantage of this insurance approach. He was quite sure by now that those companies being subsidized for their claims wouldn't be eligible.

This could be another dead end as far as solving his own insurance problems—but he still held onto a glimmer of hope.

CHAPTER 7

"I see another hand up in the back," Bill said.

"How does this PBI approach eliminate the subsidy problem you mentioned in the beginning?" asked a young woman in a floral jacket. "Isn't it the nature of insurance to share risk with others?"

"You folks are getting right to the heart of it," Bill replied. "This answer will bring more clarity to the whole concept." He turned to the whiteboard and, at the top, wrote two columns of words:

Predictable	**Unpredictable**
Manageable	**Unmanageable**
Frequent/Small	**Severe**

"What I'm about to describe," he explained, "are the central principles of PBI. The first is *what types of risks* are shared, and the second is *with whom* do you share the risks and why.

"Using the jargon of SBI, when you buy traditional, conventional, or guaranteed-cost insurance, you transfer all of your risks to the insurance carrier minus a small deductible. In most cases, you're trading dollars back and forth with your insurance company because your claims fall into this category in the column on the left." Bill swept his hand down the side of the left column. "You have a certain number of these claims every year that are predictable and manageable. However, for a financially sound company that has a strong balance sheet, it makes no sense to transfer these risks.

"In every form of PBI," he continued, "*you* become the insurance company for the frequent and manageable claims. For some companies, this means you pay the first 100,000 dollars of each and every claim. For another, it might be 500,000 dollars or even a million. The key here is you're not insuring for claims you can afford to pay yourself—*and* you're not *subsidizing* the small claims of others. Needless to say, your premium drops dramatically when you structure your insurance this way."

Tim could sense the passion and excitement in what Bill was saying. So could the others. As he looked around, all he saw was rapt attention. Whoever thought insurance could be the highlight of the day?

"But that's not all," said Bill, highly focused on his audience. "When you get in a PBI program, you can go either of two ways. You may want to pay all your predictable claims and transfer the more serious stuff to an insurance company. *Or* you could form a small insurance company with like-minded business owners who are all financially sound and safety-conscious.

"But you can't get into one of these PBI deals unless you have a strong balance sheet *and* a strong safety culture. First, you have to prove you can pay your own losses, which is the financially sound part. Second, you have to prove you *won't* have many losses and any you do have aren't likely to be severe. That's the safety part."

YOU HAVE TO PROVE YOU CAN PAY YOUR OWN LOSSES.

Bill concluded, "Maybe now you can see why it's called Performance-Based Insurance. In the simplest terms, it costs you 30 to 35 cents of the premium dollar to administer one of these PBI programs. The other 65 to 70 cents is yours to pay claims. If you don't *have* any claims, all the money becomes yours to keep. Therefore, the net cost of your insurance is based on your company's *performance*.

"Now, depending on the type of program you choose, you may be subsidizing a low layer of losses from others, but for the most part, your company's own individual claim performance determines your premium.

"And when you share risk only with the safest companies, you'll see another dramatic decrease in the cost.

He asked audience members to look at the chart on the screen. "To make this easier to visualize, I brought an example from a fellow member in my group captive, which is a form of PBI I'll explain later. This member has been in our program for four years and produced good results.

PBI Example

	08-09	09-10	10-11	11-12	
Go In Premium	431,047	415,235	424,960	445,602	
Claims	(7,973)	(78,993)	(157,752)	(172,207)	
Risk Sharing	(53,269)	(18,614)	(5,239)	(10,525)	
Investment Income	24,456	30,127	14,284	(2,500)	
Admin Cost	(152,727)	(146,752)	(146,510)	(162,687)	Total 4 Yrs
Equity	241,534	201,003	129,743	97,683	669,963
Net Cost	189,513	214,232	295,217	347,919	1,046,881
Maximum Premium (potential liability to reflect worse case claim scenario)	608,146	576,862	609,854	691,576	

Average Annual Net Cost	261,720
Last SBI Premium (07-08)	425,615
Average Annual Savings	39%

YOU CAN'T GET INTO ONE OF THESE PBI DEALS UNLESS YOU HAVE A STRONG BALANCE SHEET AND A STRONG SAFETY CULTURE.

"Down here," he indicated the lower right corner, "you can see that the last year the company had an SBI program was 2007-08. That year, it paid $425,615 in premiums. Since then, the 'Go In' premium to the captive has been in the same range as the SBI. But let's look at the chart carefully. In the first two years of having PBI, the company averaged less than half the SBI premium, showing a net cost of 189,513 dollars and 214,232 dollars respectively. Even in its worst year so far—2011-12—the cost of 347, 919 was almost 20 percent less than the 2007-08 SBI cost of 425, 615. As you can see, the average annual savings in the years since then is almost 40 percent.

"Another way to look at this is to compare the savings over two years. In this example, if you subtract the average annual net cost (261,720) from the last SBI premium (425,615), it's 163,895 dollars. If we take that savings over two years (163,895 times 2), it totals 327,790 dollars. That means we can, in effect, pay for two years and get the third year free AND have money left over."

As the speaker looked out at the audience, he saw some people shaking their heads and whispering to those sitting nearby. Others were frantically writing down the numbers.

Bill said, "Anyone who would like a copy of this chart, just throw a business card up here and write 'Graph' on it. I'll get it out to you." Then he walked closer to the screen.

"I want to point out one important line on this. Like most things in business, when there is a big payoff, there is also risk. If you look at the 'Maximum Premium' line, you will see there is a significant upcharge if you have a bad year. This is why safety is so important. In my company, I've only hit the Max once before I learned of the importance of safety. The formula for the Max is based off the Go In premium, and you know that exact amount up front. The difference between the Go In and the Max is secured by a Letter of Credit. And if you do incur a Max penalty, you can pay it over three years in annual installments. "Any questions?" asked Bill.

A gentleman in a blazer stood up at the back of the room and asked, "How realistic are these numbers? Have you shown us a best case scenario?"

Bill smiled and responded, "Believe it or not, I chose this example because it's in the middle of the pack. I didn't want to show you my company's numbers because they might not be realistic for most of you. In reality, my Go In premium is over $1.2 million and my average net cost is $500,000."

WHEN THERE IS A BIG PAYOFF, THERE IS ALSO RISK. THIS IS WHY SAFETY IS SO IMPORTANT.

Someone off to the side yelled, "This arrangement you've shown us sounds like self-insurance. I've been told my company is way too small for that, and I pay 750,000 dollars a year for my insurance."

Bill nodded. "It does sound like self-insurance, doesn't it? Without getting too technical—remember I'm a wholesaler and not an insurance expert—very few companies self-insure. Even the largest Fortune 500 companies have a PBI program that features the characteristics I described. Now, depending on their size, they might pay the first million or even first 100 million of every claim. But they're still transferring the truly catastrophic and severe claims to an insurance company. *And* they aren't sharing much with other companies."

THIS SOUNDS LIKE SELF-INSURANCE. I'VE BEEN TOLD MY COMPANY IS WAY TOO SMALL FOR THAT.

He went on to say, "I'd like to make another brief comment about the concept of self-insurance. I doubt there's any company represented in this room that has bought every type of insurance available. Even some of the common forms of insurance today such as Directors and Officers Insurance, Pollution Insurance, and Employment Practices Liability Insurance weren't available 20 or 30 years ago.

"There are always risks a company faces when no insurance is available, although that has changed recently. If we have enough time, I'll explain a new concept at the end of my talk today.

"But actually, many of the most popular forms of PBI are provided by conventional insurance companies—particularly for larger companies.

I'd like to add here that many types of insurance coverage simply aren't amenable to PBI treatment."

Bill appeared satisfied that his audience members were tuning into his message and trusting his information. With self-assurance, he walked over to a small table and poured himself a glass of water.

CHAPTER 8

"What other questions do you have?" he asked those in the audience.

As one member stood up to speak, Tim wondered if she might ask the question that finally stumped Bill—one that would prove the PBI concept to be flawed. He certainly didn't want Bill to be embarrassed at his first meeting, but he sensed that the people in the room thought PBI sounded too good to be true.

The member who'd stood up was a woman who owned a trucking company. Tim remembered her as being razor sharp in a presentation she'd given at the last Centennial meeting.

"I can't believe I haven't heard of this," she stated in a non-offensive tone. "Can you explain a little more how you learned about PBI 20 years ago and why the rest of us sound like we just fell off a turnip truck?" Everyone chuckled.

Bill smiled broadly from the stage. He seemed to know this question was coming and was prepared for it. Certainly, he must have known that smart business people pride themselves on being in the know. Maybe he would let them peek into the magic box of PBI.

"Okay," Bill said, accepting the woman's challenge. "You asked for it."

He went to a flipchart he'd prepared ahead of time. "My guess is many of you have heard of PBI programs but don't know it. Why? Because most of them are disguised in so much insurance jargon, they're misunderstood and misrepresented."

He flipped over the first blank page to reveal a long list of names:

Risk Retention Group
Baseball Retro
Retention Plan
Pure Captive
Self-Insured Retention Plan
Paid Loss Retro
Participating Dividend Plan
Safety Group
Group Captive
831(b)
Large Deductible
Association Captive
Heterogeneous Captive
Homogeneous Captive

MOST PBIS ARE DISGUISED IN SO MUCH INSURANCE JARGON THEY'RE MISUNDERSTOOD AND MISREPRESENTED.

"By show of hands again," Bill asked, "who's heard of any of these types of insurance programs?"

Some were tentative and looked confused, but 50 percent or more raised their hands.

"My insurance broker came up with PBI™ because he was tired of the confusion created by the insurance industry around these concepts. About 20 years ago, he put me in a Group Captive Program. But at the time, we also considered a Large Deductible Program. A couple of years ago, he came up with this umbrella term for all these types of structures. He called the concepts 'PBI' in a trade journal article he wrote. Frankly, the insurance industry is hidebound and hasn't paid much attention to his new terminology. Maybe in another 20 years."

WHAT DO YOU THINK WOULD HAPPEN IF ALL THE GOOD COMPANIES JUMPED OUT OF THE TRADITIONAL INSURANCE POOL, LEAVING ONLY THE BAD COMPANIES?

Chuckles of understanding came from the audience.

Bill then pointed to his flipchart list. "Some of these concepts are old and mature while others are relatively new, but they all work the same way. The ultimate net cost of the insurance is based on the individual claim *performance* of the company or, in some cases, the group of companies or a combination of individual and group performance.

"But I want to go back to something I touched on earlier," he said, walking toward the front of the stage.

"Generally speaking, the insurance companies and their agents would rather sell SBI than PBI. Think about this for a moment. We talked about risk sharing and how the companies with low claim levels subsidize those with high claim levels. What do you think would happen if all the good companies jumped out of the traditional insurance pool, leaving only the bad companies? You got it. The system would get very expensive for all those remaining." Bill let this sink in.

Tim imagined that if no one was left to subsidize his costs, his premiums would be even higher. Ouch! Never mind the system—his *company* would self-destruct! But if his was one of the bad ones being subsidized, how could he ever tame this insurance monster and become one of the good ones? If no one asked this question soon, he'd have to stand up himself. He didn't want to reveal his problem and hoped he wasn't the only one who felt this way.

Bill continued, "The insurance industry isn't the only group hiding the truth about PBI. Accountants and lawyers contribute to the misunderstanding as well. Most of these professionals are unfamiliar with the PBI concepts, yet as trusted advisors, they're consulted by business owners. In many cases, their conservatism or ignorance leads them to advise against it.

"So you might be thinking there's a good reason they advise against it. Maybe PBI is great for some but a bad idea for most. Well, I'm here to tell you it's actually the opposite—not a good idea for some but *great* for sophisticated companies that have a strong safety culture."

CHAPTER 9

Bill sipped more water and began again. "Permit me to go on a small tangent here. Has anyone ever heard of the term *captive* insurance company? As you can see, I listed some variations of it here on the flipchart," he said, pointing to the captives on his list. A small group of hands went up.

"Sounds weird, doesn't it? Captive insurance company. To many, it's a scary and confusing term, but it shouldn't be. These companies have been around a long time, and most Fortune 500 companies have one. The easy definition for *captive*—and how its name is derived—is that it's a subsidiary of an organization formed to insure the risks of its parent. It's 'captive' to its parent. Sounds simple enough, right?

"But what scares a lot of people is that, until recently, most captive insurance companies were based or 'domiciled' on offshore islands. Bermuda is the biggest, then Cayman Islands, Guernsey, Barbados, British Virgin Islands, and so on. From reading the newspapers, people think these islands are offshore tax havens for the rich and powerful. That may be, but starting in 1962 in Bermuda, they've also become worldwide centers for the specialized form of insurance company called captive. Bermuda alone hosts almost 1,000 of these companies. And more than 5,000 exist worldwide.

"Who reads the Forbes 400 wealthiest people list every year?" Bill asked rhetorically. "Two guys are always near the top of that list: Bill Gates and Warren Buffet. Do you know what businesses Warren

Buffet's holding company Berkshire Hathaway has its biggest holdings in?" Bill waited for a response. No hands went up.

"Insurance," he said, answering his own question.

"Know why? Over the years, it's proven to be one of the greatest ways to accumulate wealth—particularly if you're a smart investor like Mr. Buffet. If you had your own captive insurance company, you'd take in lots of premium and invest it over a multi-year timeframe until all of your company's losses are paid.

"As some of you may know, with insurance company accounting, every time a claim occurs, a reserve is established. Even though it can take 5 to 10 years for a liability or workers' comp claim to be fully paid, an insurance company can take a tax deduction for the full amount of the claim the year it happens. And the money set aside to pay the claim gets invested until it's paid out. Most captives have been formed outside the U.S. because the interest earned can be tax-deferred, thus compounding the benefit. Not surprisingly, many wealthy families own their own insurance companies—the PBI kind.

WHAT SCARES A LOT OF PEOPLE IS THAT, UNTIL RECENTLY, MOST CAPTIVE INSURANCE COMPANIES WERE BASED OFFSHORE.

"You know, captives are becoming more popular all the time, and they aren't all offshore. The first onshore captive was formed in Vermont in the early '60s. Now Vermont has as many as 600. In fact, I was recently told that almost 30 U.S. states have now passed laws allowing captives to be formed in their jurisdictions."

Bill scanned the eyes of those in the audience. Tim assumed he wanted to see if he still had their interest. Apparently satisfied, he continued to talk.

"The last 30 to 40 years have seen a major transformation in the way business insurance is purchased. To use industry jargon, any insurance that was non-SBI or non-conventional was put in a category called Alternative Risk Transfer or ART. Well, now the *alternative* has become the *conventional* because more than 50 percent of all worldwide business insurance premium is PBI, not SBI."

Hearing this fact shocked Tim. He looked around. Others appeared perplexed, too. *How could so many of them not be participating in a type of insurance that had become so commonplace?*

Bill seemed to sense the confusion and offered an explanation. "You have to remember," he said, "I'm talking about the amount of premium and not number of businesses. Those multi-nationals pay large amounts for insurance, even when it's been converted to a PBI program."

Someone in the front row stood up and asked, "Bill, you said earlier you're a wholesaler and not an insurance expert. How did you learn all this stuff? You sound like you know a lot more than *my* agent." Everyone laughed.

"Thanks for the compliment," replied Bill, smiling. "I know so much because I have to. I'm part owner of an insurance company and have been for 20 years. Twice a year, I get together with my 300 co-owners for two days and make decisions regarding the operation of our insurance company. We listen to consultants and outside speakers, and over the course of that time, I've learned a lot about how insurance works.

"Now, I don't want you to think I went out and started my own insurance company. I own part of what's called a group captive. Typically, group captives are formed by consultants who put all the pieces together and then invite companies like mine to join. Insurance brokers familiar with the concept are the distribution force. They find new members and then provide risk-reducing services on an ongoing basis. Our PBI company started in 1996, and it just recently achieved the status of the largest group captive in the world in terms of members."

Well, I'll be damned, thought Tim. Here, I'm being victimized by the insurance system while Bill *owns* his own insurance company.

INSURANCE IS ONE OF THE GREATEST WAYS TO ACCUMULATE WEALTH—PARTICULARLY IF YOU'RE A SMART INVESTOR LIKE WARREN BUFFET.

Desperate for an idea that would help his company, he still didn't know if he could take advantage of this one. But hearing all this hype about PBI and how common it was, Tim couldn't stand it anymore. He stood up.

"Bill, I'm likely not the only one, but I've had some tough claims recently, and at least right now, I'm probably one of those companies being subsidized. My guess is that PBI isn't for me, but I'm still unsure."

"Potentially," began Bill in response, "PBI is for everyone meeting the 100,000-dollar premium threshold. However, right now you might not be 'PBI-ready.' Remember earlier we talked about the two critical elements of PBI—the type and size of risks shared and with whom you share those risks?"

Tim nodded.

"Well, imagine you're a part owner of a group captive form of PBI like I am," said Bill. "Because you have risk-sharing—and I'll explain in a moment why this is important—you want to be sure you're sharing risk with the safest companies you can find. That way, you'll incur minimal incremental cost for the losses of others. That's how our members want it, and I'm sure if you were making the rules, you'd want it the same way.

"By the way, in case you're wondering why you have to share risk at all, our friends at the IRS demand it. It clearly states in the IRS tax code that a company can take a full deduction for the expense of business insurance. Although the code provides no definition for insurance, court cases have clarified it. You have to satisfy two rules to take the tax deduction: risk transfer and risk distribution. These are obvious in the conventional SBI model—that is, you transfer all your risk to an insurance company and it's then distributed among all the insured companies in the portfolio."

Bill again looked out over his audience—maybe checking for glassy eyes—and then went on. "What about PBI models? They differ a bit in how they satisfy the IRS, but let me explain how it works in a PBI program like ours.

"At the start of the year, the actuary calculates your premium based on your loss history. Then your premium is broken down into the fixed costs to run the company plus a premium component for frequency losses. These are made up of those under 250,000 dollars and, for severity losses, those over 250,000 dollars. To the extent your actual losses are higher than the estimate pegged by the actuary, some of the excess premium you owe is offset by contributions from other members.

"The members with the losses are also penalized, so yes, they have skin in the game. It's a simple formula and everyone knows what the maximum potential is. On average, you pay 5 percent annually for other members' losses. If you have a bad year—and everyone will from time to time—your penalty premium spreads out over three years."

By now, the attendees were taking notes, most of them nodding with understanding. The PBI concept was becoming clearer.

I'M BEING VICTIMIZED BY THE INSURANCE SYSTEM WHILE BILL OWNS HIS OWN INSURANCE COMPANY.

CHAPTER 10

Tim then posed a follow-up question. "At what level of losses will a company be rejected from membership?"

"Great question," Bill responded. "A lot of variables come into play, but it's safe to say a 50 percent loss ratio is the cutoff. That's your total losses divided by the total premium paid over a five-year period into a traditional SBI program. In group captives for which I've seen results, the long-term average is well below 50 percent.

"Remember, these are safe companies to begin with. When they earn all the profit on their premium instead of giving it to the insurance company, they take safety even more seriously. The consultant who manages my insurance company also manages one for transportation risks like school buses, limousines, and motor coaches. I recently saw their results. Their six-year loss ratio was 33 percent.

"Tim, it sounds like you probably aren't *PBI-ready* right now, but you could be very quickly. The key is to improve your safety record."

Bill then walked to the side of the stage and sat down in a chair. His lively demeanor changed to a solemn one. Tim feared he had somehow disturbed the flow of the presentation. He wished Bill would resume in his animated way.

Then Bill said, "I want to tell you a personal story that greatly affected my life and how I run my company. Unfortunately, something tragic had to happen.

"We were in the middle of the second year of our PBI program. Things had been going well and our losses were low. Now, I know we were just lucky because I was young and naive and all I wanted was to grow, grow, grow. Paying special attention to safety never occurred to me.

"One afternoon, I was coming back to our main warehouse after a sales call. As I drove into our parking lot, I saw an ambulance with its lights flashing and attendants loading a stretcher into it. I imagined the worst. The blood drained from my face. I sped up so I could talk to the attendants before they left."

At the thought of an injured worker, Tim started to sweat. He'd been there too. He looked around the room and anxious faces stared up at Bill. This wasn't heading for a good ending.

"I jumped out of my car," continued Bill, "but the attendants motioned me away and sped out to the interstate. The hospital was 10 minutes away.

"My warehouse foreman had blood splattered on his clothes and looked as if he'd seen a ghost. I frantically asked what happened.

WHEN THEY EARN ALL THE PROFIT ON THEIR PREMIUM, THEY TAKE SAFETY EVEN MORE SERIOUSLY.

"'Mickey Lane, one of our drivers,' my foreman told me. 'He'd just finished his shift and came in to check on deliveries for tomorrow. He wasn't paying attention. Jack had a big load on his forklift and was backing up to load a semi. Jack ran over something, the load tipped, and the whole thing came crashing down on Mickey's legs.'

MY WAREHOUSE FOREMAN HAD BLOOD SPLATTERED ON HIS CLOTHES AND LOOKED AS IF HE'D SEEN A GHOST.

"I asked if Mickey was conscious. Did they think he was going to make it?

"'He was conscious and in a lot of pain, but I'm afraid he couldn't feel his legs,' my foreman said."

We were all on the edge of our seats now. Bill continued with the story. "Here I was, a fairly new business owner in an insurance program that rewards low losses, and I may have just experienced the worst loss of all. I'll admit to you folks that, although I was worried about Mickey, I was probably more focused on the financial loss. The unimaginable had happened.

"Mickey ended up a paraplegic. I was called before my captive's safety committee to give a full account. Fortunately, they didn't throw me out. But that experience changed my life.

"Mickey had a wife and two young kids at the time. He had practically his whole life ahead of him and in one moment it all changed—and not for the better."

Bill stood up again. Tim could sense that retelling this story had triggered old emotions. He wondered how his colleague had dealt with this tragic accident.

But he soon heard the passion returning to Bill's voice. "I started interviewing safety managers the very next week," he said. "In addition, I started reading everything I could get my hands on about worker injuries. I had long conversations with our captive's head of safety. No way we were going to repeat this tragedy on my watch. I wanted to be the safest company in my industry. And for the first time, it wasn't about the money. It was about the *people*, my most valuable resource. I wanted to send them home every night just as healthy as when they arrived for work in the morning.

"Fast forward to today. I have 600 employees, and we haven't had a lost-time injury in three years."

You could hear gasps of disbelief coming from everywhere in the room. Tim didn't quite know what that meant or how good it was, but he could tell it must be a remarkable achievement.

"My Experience Mod Rate or EMR is .62." More gasps and whispering. Tim could benchmark this statistic; it was less than half his current 1.45. And even though Bill was talking about safety, all Tim could think of was how much money he'd save if his EMR was .62.

"Every one of my 600 employees knows that safety is the most important cultural value in our company," said Bill. "New hires are taken through a safety orientation by me personally. Our safety committee meets every single week. We have a safety manager for every one of our five warehouses and another just for our fleet. All of our warehouse staff and our drivers are taught safe lifting procedures, and these are reinforced daily. In addition, we use mechanical devices as much as possible. We even teach safety classes to our customers.

"I could go on and on about safety," he added, "because for all of us, our people are our most valuable resource, and paying attention to safety keeps them productive.

"So don't wait for tragedy. Invest in safety today. I hope I've convinced you that PBI is the only way to buy some types of business insurance, typically workers' compensation, general liability, and auto. When you combine a safe work environment with PBI, you get high productivity and low costs. That's a winning combination where I come from.

"I need to warn you, though. Creating a safe work environment isn't an overnight job. It took me years. My peers tell me it's taken them years, too. The rewards may be down the road, but you have to decide and start *today*. Otherwise, you'll be stuck in the world of SBI for as long as you own your business."

MICKEY ENDED UP A PARAPLEGIC. THAT EXPERIENCE CHANGED MY LIFE.

CHAPTER 11

Bill stopped a moment and looked as if he couldn't find the right words. Then he said firmly, "I need to tell you why I think safety is often ignored. Let me put a sharper point on this issue.

"Do I think employers don't care about their employees and whether they get hurt? No. I'm not that cynical. Do I think they're often down in the weeds watching how injured workers recover and witnessing the damage to their lives and families? They probably aren't. Most employee injuries are represented by numbers on a spreadsheet when your broker comes by at renewal time to explain why your premiums are going up."

Bill paced back and forth across the stage as he talked. "The real reason safety is ignored? *Because the insurance pricing mechanism often ignores your company's safety record.* When insurance markets are soft—as they are during 80 percent of the years in a market cycle—insurance underwriters want to maintain market share, so they ignore injuries and accidents to a great degree. Business owners react to that by going out to bid. If the underwriters don't care about the owners' accident experience, the owners find the one company underwriter who cares the least and will offer the lowest price. My broker says that, in this scenario, it's the *stupidest underwriter* who wins. That means whoever underprices the premium the most gets the business."

THE REAL REASON SAFETY IS IGNORED? BECAUSE THE INSURANCE PRICING MECHANISM OFTEN IGNORES YOUR COMPANY'S SAFETY RECORD.

Once again, Bill asked for a show of hands. "Who goes out to bid every year?" Tim slowly and haltingly raised his hand—but he wasn't alone. About 20 other participants raised theirs, also. "How about every two years?" Another 20 or so. "Every three years?" Tim figured everyone had raised a hand by now.

"I'll bet that when you go out to bid," Bill continued, "you see your premium go down by enough that you think it was worth your time." People nodded their heads. Then he asked the crowd, "What are some of the reasons you go out to bid?"

"To keep the insurance carrier honest."

"To keep my agent honest."

"Make sure I have the best coverage."

"To uncover new ideas, although it looks like everyone's been hiding PBI," said a woman in front. Laughter followed.

"I have to stay competitive, and insurance is a big line item. I negotiate it hard, just as I do with all my vendors," replied a man in the second row.

"All reasonable answers," Bill responded. "However, I bet if I looked at your data over a 10-year period, I'd find you're not getting the results you think you are."

Bill was confronting a large group of smart business owners with a strong contradictory point of view. As Tim looked around, he could see scowls on some faces and signs of outright anger and disagreement on others.

"What do you mean?" someone from the back finally asked.

"It's simple," replied Bill. "I don't want to make any enemies, so if this doesn't apply to you, ignore it—but be honest with yourself. Cheap insurance allows you to *avoid* safety. It takes the focus off the non-insurance costs related to accidents and injuries. It gives you a false sense of complacency that you're saving money. Cheap insurance is the devil tempting you with an inexpensive and easy solution . . . and it destroys companies!" Bill's voice slowed down for emphasis.

Tim was astounded that Bill used such bold words—not typical at a Centennial presentation. Right then, you could have heard a pin drop. I bet Bill's sponsor is squirming in his chair, he thought. Where was he going with this? Did he have to make the members feel foolish to get his point across?

CHEAP INSURANCE IS THE DEVIL TEMPTING YOU WITH AN INEXPENSIVE AND EASY SOLUTION . . . AND IT DESTROYS COMPANIES!

Then Bill spoke, quietly this time. "I knew a roofing contractor in Florida. One day, an employee fell from 20 feet headfirst into a tar kettle with tar heated to over 500 degrees. The financial and emotional cost of that injury caused the company to close.

"I also knew a welder for a plumbing contractor who burned down all or part of two homes due to his sloppy work. Insurance costs became so high, his company never recovered.

"And I knew a lumber manufacturer with little regard for safety in a highly hazardous industry. One day, a blade flew out of a machine and sliced the operator in half. That company never recovered financially either."

Tim sensed Bill's passion building. He was being sincere without being self-righteous. By now, everyone knew Bill had made mistakes by underestimating the importance of safety. That, in fact, had made him an evangelist for his cause. But in this situation, he just wanted people in his audience to "get" it.

"If you focus on cheap insurance, you won't invest in safety," Bill repeated. "You won't understand the operational cause and effect of accidents. As a result, your behavior relative to accidents and injuries will all be reactive. You won't build a culture that reinforces safe behavior and operations. Then it's only a matter of time before you have a disastrous and expensive year. In fact, you could be shutting down, too.

"The way insurance is sold to businesses is based purely on premium cost. Insurance brokers call on CFOs or owners. Insurance costs are displayed on a spreadsheet and the lowest cost wins. Rarely are the operational aspects of the company considered. Rarely are operational people consulted. Yet it's the operations of the company that are being insured, and it's the operations that cause the accidents that determine the cost of insurance. If safety is considered at all, the responsibility shifts to the safety manager or another operational person who has no authority to influence overall safety or change the culture.

"So," Bill said, pausing, "if you want to have the advantages of PBI, the first step is for you, as owner or CEO, to become the chief safety officer. You have to live it and breathe it every day in your culture just as you do the other core values that make yours an excellent company. I know that none of you would be sitting here today if you weren't 'best of class' in your respective industries. So why not be 'best of class' in safety?

IF YOU FOCUS ON CHEAP INSURANCE, YOU WON'T INVEST IN SAFETY

"PBI tends to put safety under the microscope. Remember, it only costs 30 to 35 cents of the premium dollar to run your insurance company. The other 65 to 70 cents are yours to pay claims. Some of our members have NO claims in a whole year. In the past 20 years, *five times* I've had NO claims during a whole year."

Tim could see the shock on the faces of his fellow conferees. NO claims? Bill was showing them a world they'd never seen. The magic box had been opened. How many members would pursue this idea? Tim wondered.

"Think about the numbers here for a moment," Bill suggested. "Your annual premium is 400,000 dollars. It costs 35 percent or 140,000 dollars to run the insurance company. You have 30,000 dollars in claims. The balance left for you is 230,000 dollars.

"Don't go out to bid any more. Invest in safety and *make* money on insurance. I'll let you use your imagination to figure out how much better your company productivity will be if no one gets hurt."

With his company experiencing a year of serious claims, Tim could better see how this would contribute to having to close his doors. Bill's message really hit home.

DON'T GO OUT TO BID ANY MORE. INVEST IN SAFETY AND MAKE MONEY ON INSURANCE.

CHAPTER 12

Now, Tim felt depressed. He barely had enough cash to cover his current fixed expenses, much less add safety managers. Then he considered his personal involvement and the extra time it would take to change his culture. His immediate thought was *not this year.* When things turned around, he promised he'd invest for sure.

Bill then asked the group, "Is everybody okay if I run over on my time a bit? I'd like to quickly mention two other ideas of a similar nature that could save all of you money. However, this might make us a little late to lunch."

A few stood up to leave. Tim recognized them as old timers who'd probably had enough new ideas for one day. Those still seated nodded their assent.

"Because I've already provided the framework, you'll get these quickly. The first relates to health insurance. I'm not going to ask you to raise your hands because I know everyone in this room is averaging double-digit annual rate increases. But would you be interested in a way to flatten those increases?"

"Absolutely!" "We sure would!" "Let's hear it!" rang out from the assembled business owners.

TIM BARELY HAD ENOUGH CASH TO COVER HIS CURRENT FIXED EXPENSES, MUCH LESS ADD SAFETY MANAGERS.

"You've probably heard of self-funding for health insurance," said Bill. "If not, it works the same as PBI in that you agree to pay a certain level of frequent smaller losses and transfer the rest to an insurance company.

"The trouble with traditional self-funding is that you can have great volatility. And you can't control the health of your employees and their family members the way you can a work environment. One major illness and your premiums could really spike.

"In my captive is a guy who always seems to be the first to learn about new insurance ideas. He explained a new variation on self-funding that carries much less risk. Instead of only you and your stop-loss carrier, you have a middle layer of risk with a group captive, and all the businesses share in that layer. I just joined, and the model I've seen shows my premium flat after five years. That will save my company millions.

"If you're interested in hearing more, write 'Health Captive' on the back of your business card and throw it on the stage when I've finished.

"Furthermore," he added, "just like the safety component with PBI, this program has a wellness component. When sharing a layer of risk with others, all participants want to know that the other member companies are doing their best to maintain a healthy workforce. This can be accomplished by introducing a smoking cessation program or an annual health risk assessment, for example. These days, the wellness business is growing exponentially. It offers self-diagnostic tools, online resource portals, health coaches—and the menu keeps expanding.

"Know that the insurance won't get cheaper. Smart companies will self-fund and eliminate the most serious health risk factors from their employee populations. I say it's a win-win—good for them and good for you. Just as PBI has become a dominant force in property and casualty insurance, I believe it will come to dominate employer health insurance for any company with more than 100 employees.

"Earlier, I said I'd learned a lot about safety when I joined my first captive. Now, I'm learning a lot about wellness," Bill said with enthusiasm. "According to Department of Health and Human Services 2010 data, between 70 and 75 percent of health care costs result from preventable illnesses. Most of these can be attributed to poor health choices such as unhealthy diets and physical inactivity. Current studies show that $73.1 billion is the estimated cost of obesity in the U.S. while 51% of Americans are pre-diabetic, 41% have high cholesterol, and 37% have high blood pressure. If we can get the resources for our employees to solve these problems, our health insurance premiums will go down instead of up *and* our company productivity will skyrocket.

"And there's a direct connection to workers' compensation, too. A Duke University study concluded that obese individuals with body mass index higher than 40 had almost double the workers' comp claims of those with normal body mass index. So wellness programs reduce costs in both insurance areas. Now, isn't that a worthwhile investment?"

He paused, letting his point sink in.

"Okay, I have one more idea I think you'll love—then lunch," promised Bill with a grin.

"If these ideas save us more money," someone from the middle of the room responded, "I'll sit here right through lunch." Others laughed; several nodded. Tim could tell they liked Bill and his honest, down-to-earth delivery.

"If you look again at my list," Bill said, walking back to his chart, "you'll see 831(b). This is a section of the tax code that allows businesses to form mini-insurance companies as long as the maximum premium is 1.2 million dollars. It's one of the hottest concepts in insurance today—not only as a risk management tool, but as an estate planning or wealth transfer tool as well."

Despite a few growling stomachs, Bill had everyone's attention. He continued, "All insurance companies, including the group captive I'm in, have to pay taxes on their underwriting income. Again, that's your net result when you subtract losses and admin from premium income.

"But 831(b)s are different. If the premium is less than 1.2 million dollars, you pay taxes only on the investment income. I'll show you examples in a minute, but let me tell you how these are used. They're designed to supplement or extend existing business insurance coverage. In their simplest form, they could cover deductibles or exclusions. Second, they could provide coverage where commercial products are unavailable or unreasonably high priced. Third, you could buy many different kinds of coverage that you haven't purchased before because you didn't see a high likelihood of loss. And fourth, you could cover areas of risk that your business faces in which no commercial coverage exists. There are no laws against creating new coverage areas just because they aren't commercially available.

"Consider these examples—

Robert Phelan   61

JUST AS PBI HAS BECOME A DOMINANT FORCE IN PROPERTY AND CASUALTY INSURANCE, HEALTH CAPTIVES WILL COME TO DOMINATE EMPLOYER HEALTH INSURANCE.

"A contractor might insure against paying OSHA fines.

"A home builder might insure against construction defect claims.

"A surgeon might insure against loss of operating privileges at a hospital.

"A trucker might insure against loss of highway privileges due to DOT violations.

"Other coverage areas could be directors and officers, pollution, performance liability, product liability, malpractice, administrative action, extortion, forgery, loss of computer data . . . there's no limitation." Bill was talking faster, glancing at the clock periodically. But his listeners were still hooked.

So he continued, saying, "You choose the coverage; an actuary calculates the premium. You keep it under 1.2 million dollars. Your company gets a full deduction for the premium paid, and you pay the 35 per cent for someone to run it. Whatever is left at the end of the year—the underwriting income—you keep and pay no taxes on while the money is kept in the captive. When you take it out in a dividend distribution, you pay capital gains tax.

"As you've probably guessed by now, this is a fairly low loss ratio type of coverage, so the captive receives consistent underwriting income."

Then someone called out from the left side of the room. "How about risk sharing? If you're paying for only your own coverage, isn't the IRS going to have a problem with that?" The questioner asked smugly, as if he thought he'd be the one to finally stump Bill.

But Bill replied with the calm and authority that comes from knowledge. "All the captive consultants setting these up either have established or have at their disposal what is called a risk pool. These risk pools are set up in similar fashion so a certain layer or percentage of risk is shared with the other 831(b) participants in the pool.

"And as I mentioned earlier, these work great for wealth transfer. Most of you own closely held or family businesses. Let's say you want to make an intergenerational transfer. You set up a trust to own the stock in the insurance company. Your company pays the premium and gets the tax deduction, but the underwriting income goes to the trust. The trust can later be used to buy your company stock. You know, my son just joined me in my business, and that's what I plan on doing with him.

"Any more questions before I wrap up?" asked Bill.

"This sounds too good to be true. I imagine these are all set up offshore," someone commented.

"Actually, they're almost all being done right here in the U.S.," replied Bill. "Mine is being set up in Delaware. The administrators can't process the applications fast enough. Other states are experiencing a similar popularity of 831(b)s. This concept has a lot of traction. You'll definitely want to check it out.

"Well, that concludes my presentation," Bill smiled. "You've been a great audience, and I've certainly felt welcomed as a new member. I hope you found the material helpful and you'll use it to save money in the years ahead. Thank you."

The attendees started applauding and then the clapping intensified. Several people stood up in a standing ovation, which astonished Tim. In his five years of membership, he'd witnessed a standing ovation only once before.

Mostly, he felt proud that Bill was his friend. He hoped he could pull him aside later in the day. But at the moment, everyone was breaking for lunch as Bill gathered the business cards scattered on the stage. A lot of people were seeking more information on the health insurance concept.

That's when Tim stopped in his tracks. Maybe, just maybe, if he saved money on his company's health insurance, he could afford to hire a safety manager. A smile lit up his face. He took out a pen, scribbled "Health Captive" on the back of one of his business cards, and threw it on the stage. He had a spring in his step as he headed out the door. Maybe he'd be renegotiating his health insurance when he returned to Charleston. Maybe he could make all or part of that $180,000 increase disappear. Oh boy, was he excited. This could change everything.

CHAPTER 13

That night during cocktail hour, Bill looked casual but sharp in a bright blue blazer that was easy to spot across the room. He appeared confident as he engaged with several members crowding around him. Tim tried to get near enough so he could overhear the conversation. As he got closer, he heard a member ask Bill, "Do you think Centennial could form one of these group captives just for our own membership?"

Bill gave a big smile and said, "On my way out here, I called the consultant who runs my program and asked him exactly that. He replied that Centennial is just the type of group he'd like to work with. Now that I see the interest, I'll talk to your executive director and set up an informational meeting with your board."

Tim could hear several members sounding elated at this news as they walked toward the bar. Wow, he thought. Bill had made quite an impact. Here it was barely six hours after his presentation and the Centennial members might be forming their own insurance company. Exciting!

Then he remembered. He probably couldn't get in. He had to find out about this health insurance program first. So he waited his turn as others slowly moved away from Bill. Finally, just the two of them stood face to face. "Boy, your message sure was well received," Tim started.

"Better than I ever imagined," Bill responded. "What a great group. I'm so glad I joined. These insurance concepts aren't easy, but the members seemed to have grasped the essential elements. I hope they can get enough participation to start their own group captive."

"How many would we need?" asked Tim.

"Probably 10 to 12 businesses to start, and then build to around 30 or 40. That would be a good size to target over the first five years or so. Easily doable with Centennial."

"So Bill, tell me more about this health insurance captive," Tim asked with great interest. "I might be able to take advantage of that right away."

"I assume you're in an SBI program with one of the major carriers now. You know. Subsidy-Based Insurance. You're mixed in with everyone else," Bill reminded him.

"Oh—yeah. We're with United Healthcare," replied Tim.

"You said you were just hit with a big rate increase. Do you know if that was because of your own claims?" Bill asked.

SO BILL, TELL ME MORE ABOUT THIS HEALTH INSURANCE CAPTIVE. I MIGHT BE ABLE TO TAKE ADVANTAGE OF THAT RIGHT AWAY.

"I don't think we had any *big* losses, but I'm not sure. My broker always tells me the claim information isn't available, like he's hiding it from me."

"Maybe not," Bill said cynically. "But you should be able to get some general information. I imagine your workforce is mostly male like mine. Are they young or old?"

"I'm lucky," said Tim. "The average age of my workforce is under 40, and we still have a lot of single guys."

"You sound like a good candidate for the program. Would you like me to have my PBI broker call you when we get back?"

"That would be terrific!" Tim felt more hopeful by the minute. "This might be the idea that helps me get back on track financially."

"I'm glad I could help, Tim. And it's been great seeing you. I'd love to continue the conversation, but I promised to have dinner tonight with my sponsor and meet some of his friends, so I have to run. I've been thinking about your workers' comp situation, and I think I have an idea that might jumpstart a new direction for you. Why don't we share a cab tomorrow when the meeting breaks and I can explain then," offered Bill.

THIS MIGHT BE THE IDEA THAT HELPS ME GET BACK ON TRACK FINANCIALLY.

"I would really appreciate that. I'll meet you at the front door at one o'clock tomorrow."

Bill walked off as Tim kept thinking about what he'd just heard. He could probably pursue the health insurance idea right away *and* Bill was personally willing to help him with his workers' comp. What a day! He felt like the bright, beautiful sunset was only for him that day. He'd been living under a dark cloud long enough.

He headed for the bar to toast his good fortune.

CHAPTER 14

The morning program on Friday seemed to zip by. Tim took lots of notes on tax credits for capital equipment purchases and negotiating lower rates and fees with bankers. Still, he was distracted with thoughts of PBI and couldn't wait for the cab ride with Bill.

He jumped out of his seat at the conclusion of the program, said good-bye to a few close friends, and hustled out to the front door to call a cab. Bill walked out of the hotel just as their cab pulled up. "Let's go!" Tim called out.

The driver stashed their bags in the trunk and, before long, was heading for the interstate and the airport.

Tim simply couldn't contain himself. On the short ride to the airport, he didn't waste a second with pleasantries. "Bill, what's this idea you mentioned about jumpstarting my workers' comp program," he blurted out.

"Well," said Bill, "we're both in the same industry and all *you* have to learn is what *I've* had to learn. It would be crazy for you to reinvent the wheel. How about if I use my safety people and resources to plan a safety kickoff meeting for your entire workforce? It would probably be a half-day program. I'd give the closing speech and share my passion for safety and why it's so important. Candidly, my words and my experience will be the most powerful persuasion for your people right now—sort of like the 'consultant from out of town' concept."

Stunned with appreciation, Tim replied, "You'd really do that? Come up to Charleston for half a day and help me get started? I'm overwhelmed by your generosity! How soon can we begin?"

"We've got some work to do first, you and me. I'll send you a list of the information I'll need to analyze first."

"Whatever you need. I'll get it for you immediately," Tim assured him.

"One more thing. I have a warehouse in Jacksonville. The safety manager there is one of my best. To gain momentum with your program, you need more help from us than just a half day. How about if I send my Jacksonville guy to Charleston for one day each month? He can sit in on your safety meetings, makes observations, and provide expertise to the safety manager I'm sure you'll be hiring." Bill winked.

"I can't believe what you're saying. No one has ever done anything like that for me before. Surely, I'd have to pay you for your time."

"No payment to me, Tim," Bill said. "I just want you to promise me that you'll commit to safety at the same level I have with my company."

"You have my word," he replied solemnly.

They'd just pulled up to the curb at Southwest—time for Tim to get out of the cab. Bill stepped out with him to get a big bear hug from his colleague and friend. "I can't thank you enough," Tim said, his eyes welling up with tears. As he went to check in, he called back, "I'll be in touch next week."

EPILOGUE

Tim sat in a soft leather chair in the hotel conference room on a warm, sunny day in Grand Cayman. He'd been in the Centennial captive for five years now. The group had 50 members now and the results were improving every year.

Safety had become a core value at his company, and he sat on the safety committee of Centennial, Ltd. for a three-year term. His company had become a highly safe place to work and hadn't experienced a lost-time injury in two full years.

The general meeting's first item was a report from the chair of the safety committee. He would review results for all of its members and give an annual recognition award, naming Centennial's Safest Company.

As Tim expected, the company's results for the year were fantastic with an overall loss ratio for the group of 30 percent. He knew his firm's own results of 10 percent loss ratio had contributed to this downward trend.

At the end of the presentation, the chair said, "We have a special guest this year who's going to help me with our annual award." He walked over to the door, stepped across the hall to another conference room, then came back with Bill Sullivan.

Tim had kept in touch with Bill regularly, so he knew Bill's captive was meeting in a bigger hotel just down the beach. In fact, they had enjoyed a drink together the night of their arrival. But Bill had said nothing to him about joining the Centennial meeting. What was he doing *here*?

The safety chair introduced Bill as a board member of Optimum, Ltd. and a five-time winner of that captive's annual safety award. Everyone knew him anyway because, even though he wasn't in the Centennial, Ltd. captive, he was still a member of the Centennial Group.

"Thanks, Joe," Bill began. "It's a pleasure to join the Centennial membership today. I can still remember my first meeting in San Francisco where one of you suggested we start this captive. What a *great* idea that turned out to be. You now have 50 members, a very low loss ratio, and millions in member equity. Congratulations to everyone for what you've accomplished.

"Because of my company's long-term commitment to safety and my membership affiliation with Centennial, Joe has asked me to confer the annual safety award today. Every year, one company's safety results and overall safety accomplishments are exemplary. This year, I'm proud and happy to present the Annual Centennial Safety Award to my very good friend, Timothy Franculli."

Tim's jaw dropped. Of all the things he'd ever done in business, this had to be the most unexpected. To be called "the safest of the safe" in a topnotch group went far beyond any goal he'd imagined when he began his journey to change the safety culture of his company.

The applause was enthusiastic, as it always was when the safety award was presented. In response, Tim pulled himself together, walked up to the front of the room, and shook hands with Bill. He knew he had to say something about this man because without his friend's expertise and support, he wouldn't even be included, much less winning a safety award.

THINK NOT JUST OF OUR FINANCIAL SUCCESS BUT ALSO OF OUR VALUED WORKERS WHO RETURN HOME TO THEIR FAMILIES EACH NIGHT AFTER WORK.

Once the applause subsided, Tim began speaking to the group. "Most of you already know my story. In the beginning, my safety record was marginal, although I doubt that was the word the safety committee used when they reviewed our record," he joked. "You also know Bill was my mentor all the way, and without his support and commitment, we would never have become members of Centennial, Ltd. Bill, you're the best. Thank you." Bill smiled and nodded to acknowledge Tim's appreciation.

"And I also thank the rest of the Centennial membership. Your commitment to encouraging and supporting a strong safety culture is admirable. I'd like us to think not just of our financial success but also of our valued workers who return home to their families each night after work. It's because of Bill and the vision he set for his company and, by example, for us that hundreds of American workers are living healthy, productive lives. And they're not getting injured while working in our companies.

"On *their* behalf, thanks to Bill and all of you."

* * *

That night as Tim walked down the sandy white Grand Cayman beach with his wife, he talked with Julie about all that had happened in the last five years. "Sometimes I have to pinch myself when I think about how good our life has become," he said. "Six years ago when I went to that Centennial meeting in San Francisco, I honestly didn't know if my business would survive or if we could ever retire comfortably."

"I know. We were both under a lot of stress back then," Julie responded.

MY MANAGEMENT TEAM IS THE STRONGEST IT'S EVER BEEN. WE'RE IN A GOOD PLACE TO START THINKING ABOUT RETIREMENT.

"*Now* look at us," Tim went on. "Instead of coming down here for a quick two-day meeting, you and I get to spend the whole week relaxing in this tropical paradise. My management team is the strongest ever so we can get away for two months a year—and we're in a good place to start thinking about retirement. We're building increasingly more equity in our 831(b) so Tony will be able to start buying the business and continue the momentum we've built." Then he chuckled. "Just before we left, Tony was talking about adding a third warehouse. He wants to expand into the Atlanta market. His energy and enthusiasm are over the top."

"And who would ever have thought all our dreams would come true because you got us into the insurance business?" Julie added. "Thirty years ago, I thought I was marrying a humble wholesaler with one delivery truck. Now you've become a successful insurance entrepreneur."

"Creating our own insurance companies has made everything possible, hasn't it?" Tim reflected out loud. "It's really amazing. I sometimes wonder how many business owners are out there with the same problems we used to have who don't know there's a solution. Maybe when I retire, I'll become a consultant and help other companies start insurance companies. What do you think?"

"Okay, Mr. Buffet. I think we should head back to the hotel," Julie replied. "There's one more Piña Colada with my name on it."

"Drinks are on me. Let's celebrate and spend a little underwriting profit," Tim said with a big smile on his face.

IS PBI™ RIGHT FOR YOU?

If you're paying from $100,000 to $10 million in annual casualty premiums (workers' compensation, general liability, auto liability) then the answer is probably yes.

At Litchfield Insurance we're experts at tailoring the many PBI options to create the program that's right for you. Still, you may have a lot of questions about PBI so I want to offer you two ways to get more information:

1. I've set up a website with resources, FAQs and a place to sign up for more detailed information.

   www.thecostofignorance.com

2. I'm offering readers of this book a free 30-minute consultation. Email or call to schedule a time to speak. My direct number is listed below.

Bob Phelan
860-761-7201
bgphelan@litchfieldins.com
www.litchfieldins.com

ABOUT THE AUTHOR

Robert (Bob) Phelan is a 30-year veteran of the insurance industry. As chairman and CEO of Litchfield Insurance Group, he has led his firm to national prominence by providing value-added services to clients. His company was one of ten U.S. insurance brokers recognized for innovation by *Best's Review*.

Inspired by his father who introduced him to the business, he considers his clients' successes to be his greatest achievement.

Bob earned his BA from Tufts University, holds the Associate in Risk Management (ARM) designation, and is a graduate of the Buckley School of Public Speaking. He's the author of *Broke: The Broken Contractor's Insurance System and How to Fix It* and is a co-author of *Secrets of Peak Performers*.

A thought leader in his industry, Bob speaks across the U.S. and Canada about PBI and other value-added services. He was recognized by the National Alliance Research Academy as one of "The 25 Most Innovative Agents in America." *Risk & Insurance Magazine* named him one of six "Power Brokers" for the U.S. in Construction.

Bob is an Editorial Advisory Board member for *Rough Notes Magazine*, the largest trade journal for the insurance brokerage industry.

www.ingramcontent.com/pod-product-compliance
Lightning Source LLC
Chambersburg PA
CBHW031402180326
41458CB00043B/6577/J